For James.

With Best wishes.

JAY JEFFERS
COLLECTED
COOL

Dressing in the Dark

LA BEAUTÉ EN VOYAG

THE ART OF BOLD, STYLISH INTERIORS
Jay Jeffers with Alisa Carroll
Principal Photography by Matthew Millman

RIZZOLI
NEW YORK

New York Paris London Milan

JAY JEFFERS
COLLECTED
COOL

To my parents, who always told me I could do anything. And to my grandmother, whose best advice was "Give a little, save a little, spend a little." I have applied that to everything in my life.

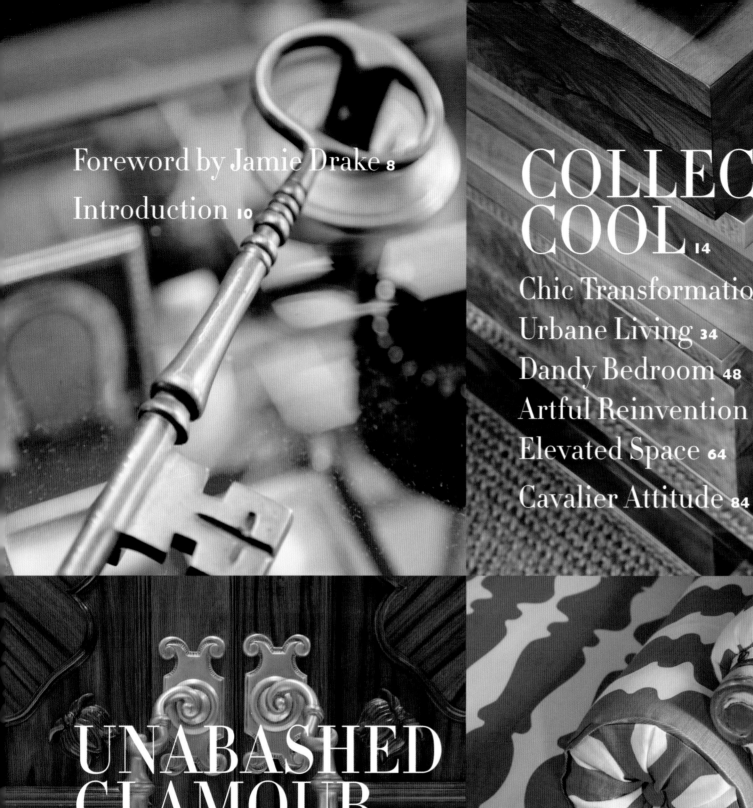

BOLD BESPOKE

CASUAL CHIC

The world of design is a magical kingdom, and sometimes one is lucky enough to enter the dream world of a true magician. Jay Jeffers is one of the most talented conjurers I know.

When I first met Jay in 2002, he had just been anointed one of the Next Wave of the country's leading young designers by *House Beautiful*. I was struck by the sophisticated, painterly spaces he created. Jay's ability to design totally contemporary interiors that embody traditional comfort is nonpareil. With his wonderful eye, he deftly mixes colors, periods, and shapes. His spaces are easy to live in, without pretension and yet always intellectually stimulating and put together with a collector's touch. Sourcing pieces new and old, custom and bespoke, his particular taste runs toward the tailored, always boldly detailed and smartly delineated.

In 2007, Jay designed a room for the *House & Garden* Hamptons Showhouse. Jay's room was bright and cheerful, and I recognized several fabrics I'd used in my own designs (I like a little color). I realized we were kindred design spirits. To celebrate the opening of the showhouse, I hosted Jay, his husband, Michael, and family and friends at my home in East Hampton. Jay brought his characteristic energy and wit to that weekend, and it's been a lasting friendship ever since.

That same personality is inherent in all of Jay's rooms. Instantly one is intrigued by the heady mélange he creates for his clients that clearly reflects their passions as filtered through his exacting eye. For all its warmth, Jay Jeffers's work is the epitome of cool . . . *Collected Cool.*

JAY JEFFERS

I decided I would be an architect at an early age. Growing up in my childhood home in a suburb of Dallas, I didn't know any architects, or what they did, exactly—but pouring over my prized cache of *Architectural Digests*, I knew I wanted to make houses that looked like that. I was constantly rearranging furniture in my room and, when I got tired of that confined space, I rearranged the furniture in our living room. Fortunately, my creativity was always encouraged by my mother, a master seamstress who made everything from clothing to bedspreads. She even upholstered the walls in my room. (She later went on to found a tech company and earn a PhD, but that's another story.)

As I grew up, however, my practical side got the better of me and I went on to study international business at the University of Texas. While there, I discovered the creativity of advertising and set out to be the next Hal Riney. Architecture and design, however, were never far away. The black-and-red décor of my freshman dorm room—complete with Nagel prints—was coveted by all, and my roommate and I were fabulous hosts.

My first job after moving to San Francisco was in the advertising department at Gap, Inc., and it was an education of riches. Ultimately, though, I felt that I needed something more expressive, intimate, and personal. I came across an interior design course, and it was love from first swatch. Art history, architecture, custom furniture, field trips to upholsterers—I was smitten with everything about it.

My first job in the industry was with Richard Witzel Design, and during my four-year tenure, I had the opportunity to learn from both Richard and the incredible San Francisco design community: Paul Wiseman, Suzanne Tucker, Gary Hutton, Leavitt Weaver, and many others were inspirations and guides. One of my major early touchstones was David Hicks—discovering his work was monumental for me. I felt like we must have been related in a past life. His pairing of modern with traditional, brilliant mixes of patterns, accessorizing, and incredible attention to detail all felt like home to me.

I ventured out on my own in 1999 with Jay Jeffers Interiors. From my own first home—where I trellised the chocolate-brown walls with pink-and-orange grosgrain ribbon—to my latest project, fun, glamour, and exuberance have been at the core of my sensibility. That might mean a high-gloss, tangerine-hued ceiling, a Gio Ponti chair upholstered in a bold stripe, or a powder room in a cheeky print. My goal is to create luxurious and livable spaces—they've just got to have a kick in their step!

Another designer I think I must be related to is Jamie Drake. Jamie's unabashed use of color and texture are beyond fabulous. I had the great pleasure of meeting him at an event in New York in 2002. We stayed in touch, and I now consider Jamie a great friend and one of the great talents of our generation. I'm honored that he agreed to write the foreword to this book.

I still love to rearrange furniture—just ask my husband—and I consider myself incredibly fortunate to be able to do it for a living. To quote the great Billy Baldwin, "Interior design is the art of arranging beautiful things, comfortably." And, I would add, fearlessly! I hope that this book, a collection of my favorite projects, inspires you to do just that.

ÉDITIONS DU REGARD

CALIFORNIA ROMANTICA

sheila metzner
form and fashion

AXEL VERVOORDT
THE STORY OF A STYLE

ASSOULINE

IKE KLIGERMAN BARKLEY
HOUSES

ROOMS
TO
REMEMBER

RICHARD
DIEBENKORN

PARISH

COLLECTED COOL

It's all in the mix. What applies to a fabulous dinner party, wardrobe, or cocktail also holds true for interiors. A captivating room is thoughtfully layered, revealing itself over time through myriad details like meticulous embroidery on a silk pillow or the shadows cast by a hand-blown glass chandelier. A successful space is more than the sum of its parts. Like Albert Hadley's red-lacquered Astor library or the lobby of the Hôtel Costes, a well-curated room takes on another dimension that makes it timeless and endlessly alluring.

A fresh mix of custom, vintage, and antique furniture is the foundation of all my interiors. One of my greatest pleasures is creating unexpected juxtapositions and watching new relationships take shape. Over the years, I've paired Jean Royère pieces with flea-market finds, Gio Ponti classics with baroque wonders, and the work of Patricia Urquiola with that of Christian Liaigre. Like the perfect guest list, the mix needs to be planned using an internal logic—a correspondence in scale, shape, color—that ensures a harmonious whole.

Ultimately, fine art, accessories, and personal objects are the soul of a room. Each piece brings its own energy to a space; it can set the mood, or disrupt it, in an unexpected but inspiring way. I have the privilege of working with many clients to curate collections of fine art and objects, and whether their prized possessions are wonderful things picked up on their travels or family heirlooms, they speak of a life well lived.

Architect Jean Nouvel argues, "Art should be created for life, not for the museum." Likewise, an interior designer's role is to create artful spaces that enliven and enrich the client's lifestyle. The goal is not a *tableau vivant* but an environment that changes and evolves. This San Francisco residence provided an opportunity to create just such a space, one that would be both stylishly set and well suited to a family on the move.

What evolved was a comfortable home with an industrial edge. We incorporated "raw" materials but always made them feel elegant. In the master bedroom, we created a rustic wall from reclaimed teak but enveloped the rest of the space in a chic cream, blue, and brown palette (the colorways are picked up in the drapes and the benches topped with khaki-and-blue velvet). Likewise, the furnishings have strong lines, but materials in a variety of textures ensure that nothing feels too severe. The rectangular side tables, for example, are covered in shagreen. The bed is enveloped in linen. And the rock crystal chandelier has edge, but when illuminated it transforms into a softly glowing sphere (naughty but nice—my favorite combination). It's a serene but sexy space.

"The blah corner fireplace got a face-lift with a book-matched veneer, granite, and a funky agate fireplace screen."

OPPOSITE: We carried the jeweled motif into the furnishings, the fabrics, and even the artwork— hence the diamond-shaped lattice of the vintage steel-and-glass coffee table, the glass teardrop light fixture, and the seven-foot charcoal drawing of a crystal chandelier by Gonzalo Fuenmayor. **RIGHT:** The gems in the screen are unexpected and very sexy. **FOLLOWING PAGES:** The oversize wing chairs are perfect for settling into with coffee and the morning paper (or for champagne and gossip); the midcentury armchairs are by Monteverdi Young. The George Smith tufted suede ottoman in robin's-egg blue picks up the teal in the back-painted custom shelves.

"Accessorize! Accessorize! Nothing looks more incomplete than a beautiful room with empty shelves."

LEFT: This sunny reading nook off the kitchen is the perfect space for dreaming up the next dinner party. The custom white lacquer shelves house the client's cookbooks and favorite *objets de cuisine*. The lounge chair is clad in Imperial Trellis fabric by Kelly Wearstler for Schumacher, and the window coverings are ivory sheers with green, blue, and yellow stripes by Designers Guild. **OPPOSITE:** Again, it is all about the juxtaposition of materials. Here, glass (the chandelier), iron (the lamp), and wood (the tamarind-tree-stump table) come together beautifully.

Design is a layering process, and each element—from the species
of wood to the finish of the paint—is equally important.

"I love the subtle— or not so subtle— tension between the organic and the polished. Here, the Hermès-orange lacquered ceiling stares down the live-edge table."

LEFT: The figuration of the Suar wood gives this tabletop beautiful flow. **OPPOSITE:** A Jean de Merry antiqued brass starburst chandelier elegantly illuminates the room; dining chairs are covered in Designers Guild fabric. Chain-link grass-cloth wall covering by Phillip Jeffries; circa 1900 Khotan rug from Tony Kitz Gallery. **FOLLOWING PAGES:** This very sporting library was previously a sterile white box.

PREVIOUS PAGES: A custom JDG (Jeffers Design Group) bed upholstered in ivory Holly Hunt fabric rests against a reclaimed teak wall. OPPOSITE AND BELOW: This is a nursery with lots of charm. A box-pleated valance and drapes in an ivory-and-dove-gray print hug a cozy window seat, and above hangs a festoon of paper pom-poms, one of my favorite elements of the room.

Like the mix of surfaces and materials in this foyer vignette, this home is all about texture, from fine art to antiques to fabrics. Throughout the house, tactile, sculptural elements converge to create a look that is sensual and drop-dead handsome. In this dining room, I love the Venetian plaster ceiling, onyx black and constellated with gold dust; the leather chandelier; the alternating panels in ebonized oak and wallpaper; and the diamond-point Italian credenza that is glamorous and a little dangerous.

In the living room and hall, a petrified-wood-and-bronze side table, Biedermeier chairs in a Chapas Textiles fabric, and a polished walnut console by Hudson Furniture showcase varied surfaces. In the bedroom, soft blue suede cloth envelops the walls. Even underfoot, Berber wool and bamboo silk rugs add texture. Ultimately, in this home, the feel is everything.

"This space is urbane, moody, and sexy. I want to slip on a smoking jacket as soon as I walk in."

PREVIOUS PAGES: A bronze Philip and Kelvin LaVerne coffee table anchors the living room. **LEFT:** A pair of red ceramic lamps add a burst of color. **OPPOSITE:** The octagonal mirror plays up the motif in the rug.

PREVIOUS PAGES: Though it looks petite, this curved settee easily accommodates two—perfect for cozying up to your neighbor at a sexy dinner party. BELOW: *Untitled* by Richard Misrach hangs above the Hudson Furniture Infinity console; Madeline Stuart Harper chairs. OPPOSITE: This vignette features an interesting combination of textures, from the linen-wrapped late-nineteenth-century French slipper chairs to the petrified-wood end table.

The Hotel Book

PREVIOUS PAGES: There's a strength to this house, and these rooms epitomize that—the bold shapes and materials like leather and bronze have muscle. **OPPOSITE:** The suede wall covering is so soft, you just want to touch the walls. The abstract painting by John DiPaolo creates a fabulous dramatic moment. **BELOW:** We designed the blue leather bed—I mean, really, what could be sexier and more sumptuous than a leather bed?

DANDY BEDROOM

From the smart tartan bed to the cultivated collection of furnishings, this is a space for a twenty-first-century dandy—the gentleman in the Thom Browne suit. We designed this space for a soul who charts his own course. When not at Clignancourt, he can be found with a cocktail at the King Cole Bar. Everywhere there are reminders of past journeys: painted archways mimic classical portals, the Gio Ponti chair—a reclaimed seat from an Italian train car—still bears its brass number plate. The cache of European treasures includes Roman busts, a heraldic mirror, and a portrait of a dandy (with great hair, of course). In the spirit of our client's disregard for convention, we carried the trompe l'oeil arches up over the molding onto the ceiling. Ultimately, this room was created for interior and exterior reflection: with mirrors from armoire to wall to table, we ensured our flâneur could contemplate his journey and, of course, look good while doing it.

BELOW: The palette juxtaposes warm burnt oranges with cool blues; we designed the custom bed and upholstered it in an orange, gray, and taupe Osborne & Little plaid. The fabulous wall treatment is by Philippe Grandvoinet. OPPOSITE: A mirrored étagère is perfect for showcasing favorite objects.

"David Hicks was the master of the tablescape. His work taught me so much about grouping accessories and being fearless about mixing sizes, shapes, colors, and periods."

PREVIOUS PAGES: This vignette mixes it up in every way—we really had fun layering patterns, colors, and periods. **LEFT:** A collection of handsome accessories tops a 1940s ormolu-mounted églomisé chest. **OPPOSITE:** A collection of vintage portraits, including one of a dandy.

This home demonstrates how collected cool can be spare. This is the only project I've done with a distinctly Eastern influence; the tone was set by the very first work of art we acquired for the home: Mike + Doug Starn's *Gyoki*. We transformed the home—originally a generic developer property—into an innovative space with a serene sensibility.

The plan is all about letting it flow. On the first floor, for example, the dining room is open to the main living area. To evoke shoji screens, we installed drapery that can be drawn to close off the kitchen and living room, creating a more intimate space. We also designed a "broken" dining table that can be separated into two pieces to maintain an open pathway through the dining room. In the master bedroom, the bespoke walnut platform bed is backed by integrated shelving that allows for more open space in the room. The soft cream, blue, and gray palette helps maintain the peaceful atmosphere (though we couldn't resist a few pops of color in the guest room).

"There's a complex composition of shapes in the living room, but because there's a consistent tonality, it feels cohesive."

A streamlined sofa paired with an undulating Asian table and a hexagonal accent table creates a dynamic juxtaposition.

"The inset shelving serves double duty as an unexpected headboard as well as a cozy spot for displaying a collection of favorite things."

PREVIOUS PAGES: The stone sculpture of the Guyan Mudra is a gesture of calm and peace, and we really wanted to express that feeling in this space. **RIGHT:** Monochromatic finishes, flooring, and bedding create a serene setting. The custom platform bed is by JDG.

The Kama Sutra Illuminated Erotic Art of India

In this sky-high Russian Hill home, floor-to-ceiling windows blur the boundary between interior and exterior. They frame a quintessential San Francisco skyline view that begins with Grace Cathedral, encompasses the Golden Gate Bridge and Bay Bridge, and ends with the Transamerica Pyramid. The apartment was originally designed by the brilliant Michael Taylor, but the pink chenille wallpaper, carpeted baths, and mirrored walls—though the height of style in their time—had run their course.

The new owners wanted a clean, modern canvas that would showcase their art collection. To coax the city's ethereal atmosphere inside, we chose a palette of grays, taupes, and white to make it look as though the fog had rolled in and taken shape. Bold, sculptural forms, from the strong silhouettes of the wing chairs to the angular lines of the floating console, also give the space wow factor.

A look this minimalist leaves no room for error. We were fortunate to collaborate with Sutro Architects, whose rigor helped ensure impeccable lines. We took the space back to the studs and opened it up by taking down all of the interior walls.

And though the look is streamlined, it's never flat or cold. We chose finishes in a range of textures from chalky whitewash to striated limestone to flamed granite.

We like to think that whether looking out of the windows or in, the view is equally stunning.

"For the passage leading to the guest room, in place of traditional doors, we designed sliding walnut panels to preserve the open flow of the space."

RIGHT: An Emerson Woelffer work in oil, roof cement, and collage adds a pop of color and texture to the main hall.

"Day or night, the views are magical."

PREVIOUS PAGES: In the very cosmopolitan living room, a circle of curvaceous wing chairs creates a glamorous focal point. A Michael Berman ottoman clad in luscious cream bouclé is a soft spot to put your feet up (shoes off, please). **LEFT:** Whether a catered dinner or Chinese takeout, everything tastes better sitting in this spot. **OPPOSITE:** The sight lines of the kitchen direct all eyes to the glittering waterfront.

"Cool can be comfy—
this room has a deep
sofa and big barrel
chairs that just beg you
to sink into them."

At every turn, this space offers something
sumptuous to the touch. Kyle Bunting hair-on-
hide covers the wall, the Gary Hutton chairs are
swathed in suede, and the rug is silk cut-pile.
When the conversation gets really juicy, guests
can nestle on the Christian Grevstad sofa
ensconced between the bookshelves. The
fabulous floating glass-and-black-walnut coffee
table is by John Houshmand.

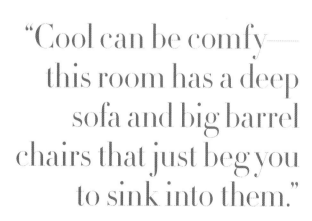

OPPOSITE: In this diaphanous space, Masatoyo Kishi's *Opus No. 61-313* adds a stroke of drama. We designed the floating bench that emerges from the white limestone slab wall, and the vintage mahogany-and-leather lounge chairs are by Raphaël Raffel. **BELOW:** I love how this ethereal gray space looks like an extension of the view.

"Even when suffused by fog, the city view is inspiring."

The master bedroom is oriented to take maximum advantage of the windows. The view from the custom walnut platform bed is unobstructed; the silver pendant lights were made with hand-blown teardrops of mirrored glass discovered at Twentieth Century Interiors. The swivel-base lounge chairs are by Mattaliano; the wool-and-linen ottoman is by JDG.

Textures and details sing throughout the home. **BELOW:** The custom JDG ottoman features a Pierre Frey fabric (top left); hand-blown glass pendant lights by John Pomp Studios (top right); Robert Motherwell's *In the Summer Sun* graces the desktop (bottom left). **OPPOSITE:** Shizue Imai's earthenware *Totem* sculpture (top center); a Murano glass Pedras vase (bottom left).

"Wrapping baths entirely in tile makes them feel sleek and luxurious."

LEFT: The guest bath is clad in stone tile. **OPPOSITE:** *Echo* by Lorraine Shemesh tops a vintage Pierre Chapo dresser.

BELOW: In this space, we kept it subdued and simple to frame the view of the neighboring neoclassical building. **OPPOSITE:** In the study, *Museum Pieces* by Catherine Wagner maintains a steady gaze on the scene.

I launched my first retail shop, Cavalier by Jay Jeffers, in 2012 as a place to share my passion for bold, uncommon home furnishings and accessories. Housed in the front of the 4,000-square-foot JDG studios, Cavalier is an integral part of the life and work of the firm. It's where we receive visitors, brainstorm, and kick back with cocktails. It's the heart of our movable feast.

My husband and coproprietor, Michael Purdy, and I wanted the atmosphere to feel like home, a place where guests would feel welcome to linger, explore, and hear the story behind each singular piece. We designed custom blackened-steel shelving to hold objects and accessories and a freestanding backlit white wall to showcase fine art. Chandeliers and fixtures are suspended like sculpture from the 18-foot ceilings. And the vignettes are always changing and evolving depending on our latest discoveries and inspirations.

But Cavalier will always be anchored by a comfy sitting area that invites lounging with a glass of wine (at Cavalier, imbibing is always strongly encouraged), because what's most meaningful to us is having a place to share what we love with old friends and new.

"Our 'Cavalier code' celebrates all things thoughtful, inspiring, and adventurous."

LEFT: This handsome sofa, with cerused oak arms and base, was the first piece I designed for my furnishings collection. I was under pressure to name the pieces, hence The Kingsley: it is named after our Cavalier King Charles Spaniel.
OPPOSITE: Meet its BFF, The Coulter, named for Kingsley's best friend. *Jacques*, an eight-by-six-and-a-half-foot oil by Jerome Lagarrigue, complements the grand scale of our space.

"A home to all things singular and luxurious, we designed Cavalier to be a space for those who take their pleasures seriously."

This vignette epitomizes Cavalier style: in front of the bespoke Kingsley sofa sits a quartet of charred-wood tables by Toronto artist Martha Sturdy. A vintage Italian bar cart is stocked with a contemporary glass decanter and tumblers by Nason Moretti.

ttfn!

"I truly believe that if you surround yourself with beauty, you will be a happier person for it."

LEFT: Our modern cabinet of curiosities: shelves stocked with art, natural objects, vintage glassware and Alex & Lee jewels enclosed in bell jars. **RIGHT:** A luxurious hand-woven leather pillow by Lance Wovens and Michelle Hatch's studded "C" pillow, custom-made for Cavalier.

BOLD
BESPOKE

The men of Milan, with their rolled-up pants and Ferragamo loafers worn without socks, are the embodiment of bold bespoke. With a confidence grounded in impeccable tailoring—from construction to proportion to fabrics—the chic Milanese are empowered to break the rules and stand apart from the crowd.

I bring that attitude to interiors, and envisioning spaces through a sartorial lens is always a huge source of inspiration for me: I've done a Burberry-inspired tartan tile backsplash to give a kitchen dash, a set of custom bronze fireplace tools to evoke the burnish of metal furnishings, and a Vladimir Kagan sofa upholstered in caramel-colored eel skin to call to mind a luxe watchband (worn outside the sleeve, of course).

And just as they say in fashion, if everyone has it, it's over! Luxury is singularity. We have a fabulous client with whom we've worked for years who said at our very first meeting, "I don't want my home to look like anyone else's." Bespoke and custom elements are essential to achieving a personalized interior. From sketching the curve of a headboard to selecting the grain and finish of the wood, we work to craft furnishings that are entirely fresh and entirely new.

Of course, having the freedom to create these objects is itself a luxury. The residences in this chapter are a credit to visionary clients who were able and willing to invest the time and resources to explore and push the boundaries of design. It's an intensely personal and creative undertaking and one I always hope lives on in these heirlooms. As the Italians say, "*Ad ogni uccello, suo nido è bello*"—every bird finds its own nest beautiful.

Crossing the threshold of this home is like exhaling deeply. Despite its grand scale, the space feels intimate and inviting—the clean lines and uncluttered rooms reflect the owners' informal lifestyle, and the spice tones establish a warm atmosphere.

This home has joyful energy, but that's not to say that decorating it wasn't rigorous work. There is incredible attention to detail in every room, from decorative painting to bespoke furnishings to tabletop accessories. As a finishing touch, a group of artists hand-painted twenty dinner settings with a custom blue-and-orange pattern of our design. When the china is paired with the client's orange Venetian glass goblets, a prismatic scene is set for entertaining.

The graphic elements in the architecture inspired us to be playful. We picked up their strong shapes, including the cast of shadows and light, in textiles and furnishings. A handwoven Tibetan wool rug with a polka-dot motif, for example, takes the seriousness out of the grand entry. Welcome to the epitome of bold bespoke.

"Vibrant works of art bring great presence to a room. I love these bold pieces by Jules Olitski and Liza Lou."

PREVIOUS PAGES: This home is all about great energy; you feel peaceful and invigorated in it. **LEFT:** In the living room, we designed the ottoman base to preserve the flow of the view; its tapered rods create the illusion that it's floating. The cushion is in a vibrant Bergamo ikat. **OPPOSITE:** The wing chair, one of a pair, is by Gio Ponti, originally designed for the legendary Parco dei Principi hotel in Rome. We reupholstered them in tangy orange and raspberry textiles. The side chairs are a midcentury-inspired JDG design upholstered in a woven gold fabric.

PREVIOUS PAGES: One of a pair of rosewood bar cabinets that flank the fireplace. Our inspiration for this gorgeous cabinet was an antique Japanese decorative box. Crafted using lacquer and inlaid with crushed pearl, the piece features a landscape we designed in collaboration with the cabinetmaker. **BELOW AND OPPOSITE:** Lyrical details illustrate the extraordinary technical range of the craftspeople who contributed to this project. From weaving and embroidery to glassblowing and metallurgy, the skills demonstrated here are a testament to the artisans and craftspeople who are the core of interior design.

OPPOSITE: The custom walnut Tresserra billiards table was handcrafted in Spain, and four strapping Spanish men escorted it to San Francisco for installation. The walls are faux-painted to look like stitched leather; we continued the detailing onto the drapes for a whimsical touch. BELOW: There is very little natural light on the lower level of the home, so we really turned up the color volume. In the theater, we upholstered the ceiling and front speaker in a raspberry Pierre Frey fabric, and underfoot is a custom-colored rug by Tai Ping. Willem Racké hand-painted the columns and the Moroccan faux-tile wainscoting. Custom embroidered throws are on hand for snuggling up on movie night.

"This black walnut headboard resembles a sweeping brushstroke; it's a fun nod to the artistry of the home."

RIGHT: A pair of groovy 1960s Italian chrome-and-Lucite petal lamps top side tables by Stratford House. The midcentury Italian chair is upholstered in a Florence Broadhurst print.
FOLLOWING PAGES: Inspired by the clean lines of the home, we designed this fabulous geometric bed and bird's-eye maple bedside tables, which are cantilevered and weighted at the bottom so they tuck underneath the bed. Though one should obviously never match art literally to décor, this painting is a playful take on the geometries of the space.

Working with clients who believe passionately in the design process drives me to create the perfect piece and to find the most inspired solution. This glorious, high-spirited San Francisco home is one of the most bespoke projects I've had the privilege to design. The project was so much fun, I think we imprinted a sense of vibrancy and joy upon it.

We designed custom elements ranging from the exquisite wood latticework that frames the second-floor sitting area to the bronze post-and-rail grand entry stairway. We also ensured that the interior architecture was impeccably tailored to the client's sensibility.

It doesn't take a village to create a home like this—it takes a small city. An entire community of artists came together to realize the vision for this property, and when it was complete, the clients graciously hosted a party for the team. The guests—just like their artistry—filled the entire home.

BELOW: Begin the bespoke. We designed the V'Soske silk stair runner to make a fabulous first impression. **OPPOSITE:** The living room features a stunning hand-stenciled-and-painted floor by Willem Racké and persimmon strié glazed walls by Philippe Grandvoinet. We designed the bespoke bronze-and-bleached walnut settee to hug the curve of the window wall.

PREVIOUS PAGES: This client obviously embraced color, and one vibrant piece in particular set the tone for the rest of the home: the humble ottoman. The lively oranges and pinks of the Pierre Frey fabric established our color story for the space. Two Murano glass floor lamps flank the ten-foot Michael Berman sofa; above hangs a Jeanne Duval still life. BELOW: We redesigned the existing hallway to create a gallery experience. A trio of paneled vestibules showcases works from the client's collection, including Ilya Zomb's *Lady of the Lake*. OPPOSITE: One of my favorite vignettes in the home brings together a lustrous art deco rosewood buffet, an antique Georg Jensen tea service, and a spellbinding Herve Van der Straeten mirror, which adds a fairy-tale quality to the scene.

118

BELOW: Highlights of fabulous details throughout the home include a pink-and-gold crushed-glass floor by Ellen Blakeley (top left). OPPOSITE: A custom lotus-detail bronze stair rail and a bespoke V'Soske wool-and-silk stair runner add to the rich feel (top center).

OPPOSITE: The hand-carved rosewood swing is an unexpected and playful touch; even the chain is custom!
BELOW: We designed the arched entrance to the sitting room, which transforms the hallway into a lovely moment. The arch and petal columns are hand-carved pickled pine with olive-green glass insets.

"This master bedroom is our take on classic elegance and all things extravagant: Murano, Fortuny, brocade, cashmere."

Upholstered in gold silk, the walls are a sumptuous canvas for superb European antiques. To the left of the bed is an Italian Balestra commode with tuxedo-striped satinwood and rosewood marquetry; to the right is a Sicilian serpentine commode in walnut. Both date to the 1700s. The circa-1920 painted French bergères are upholstered in Fortuny.

PREVIOUS PAGES: The console table was designed by T.H. Robsjohn-Gibbings for the historic Bel Air estate Casa Encantada. A glimpse into the master dressing area. **BELOW:** We wanted the "blue bedroom" to be sophisticated but youthful, so there are whimsical touches throughout. The hand-carved headboard is topped with a playful loop and upholstered in soft blue-gray velvet. Swallows swoop across the hand-painted Fromental wallpaper, and oversize poppies bloom on the drapes. **OPPOSITE:** In the same room, this very stylish spot for studying features a midcentury desk, a Lucite chair, and a 1940s blue Murano glass lamp, one of a pair.

BELOW: Sweet dreams, indeed. From ceiling to floor, this bedroom is designed entirely in candy colors. The hand-painted wallpaper is by Fromental; the custom duvet and shams are by Susan Chastain; and the etamine drapery panels are pink-and-green wide-striped silk.
OPPOSITE: How could you not feel fabulous dressing amid these golden parchment strié walls?

Every designer's home is his or her lab, and my beloved 1915 Edwardian cottage in San Francisco is the place where I began to experiment with bold color and pattern. Among other design adventures, I trellised pink-and-orange grosgrain ribbon on the bedroom walls and hand-stenciled my monogram on the drapes in an homage to David Hicks.

My home's last incarnation was handsomely quirky; a trip to Amsterdam inspired the sea change. My husband and I stayed at a lovely hotel where all the moldings were painted a beautiful taupe. I always want a home to have warmth, and I thought that meant radiant tones like gold or persimmon. But that little hotel taught me that I could achieve that feeling with cooler hues as well. Back home, when I painted over the traditional white moldings in charcoal gray, it changed the whole personality of the house. The master bedroom, now robed in subdued tones and textures, and the dining room, swathed in cream and brown, took on a dapper new look. But hello, guest room! A portrait of Abe Lincoln in hot pink took pride of place against a backdrop of acid-hued wallpaper. I couldn't completely ignore my roots!

And speaking of color, have you met our kitchen? He's the guy at the barbeque rocking the pink Lacoste pants. I love plaid, whether Burberry or Michael Bastian; friends will tell you it's a style signature of mine. Our kitchen is an ode to the power of prep.

BELOW: In the living room, I implemented my own advice with persimmon-hued walls and a hot-pink lacquer coffee table. OPPOSITE: This smart little vignette features a Paul Frankl table, a vintage weight, and an illustration by Christopher Brown.

"Whether it's a party of four or forty, everyone always ends up in the kitchen, so make it chic!"

PREVIOUS PAGES: A collection of manly portraits (including one of our dog Kingsley) adorns the dining room wall. **LEFT:** Because you see the kitchen from every space of the main floor, we wanted it to have a bold personality, hence the tartan mosaic backsplash and persimmon back-painted cabinets. **OPPOSITE:** The sitting area right off the kitchen is the perfect place to gather with friends; I designed the sofa based on an Italian antique. The painting, *Interval (2)*, is by a favorite artist, Forrest Williams. **FOLLOWING PAGES:** There are lots of personal touches in the bedroom, from the grouping of dapper objects on the dresser to the plaid bed I designed to my color-coordinated copper kicks (deal with it).

his great room is all about bespoke solutions to a challenging space. It was so architecturally alien from the rest of the home that we decided to make it feel as though it had flown in and landed on the top of the house à la *The Wizard of Oz.* We began by faux-painting steel rivets where the corners met, creating the impression that the room was fastened on. The look of hardware also inspired our industrial-chic concept, reinforced by pieces like the steel fireplace surround and steel-and-leather barn doors.

We kept the room from feeling too heavy with a sunny palette of yellows and creams. We carried this colorway into the honeycomb hair-on-hide rug, the sofa, and the 1950s Italian wing chairs. We also collaborated with local lighting designer Michael McEwen on the spectacular steel-and-glass teardrop chandelier.

Ultimately, despite the space's idiosyncrasies, we achieved harmony through pairings of opposites: vintage and contemporary pieces, light and dark hues, tough and soft materials. And that's just the mix we love at JDG.

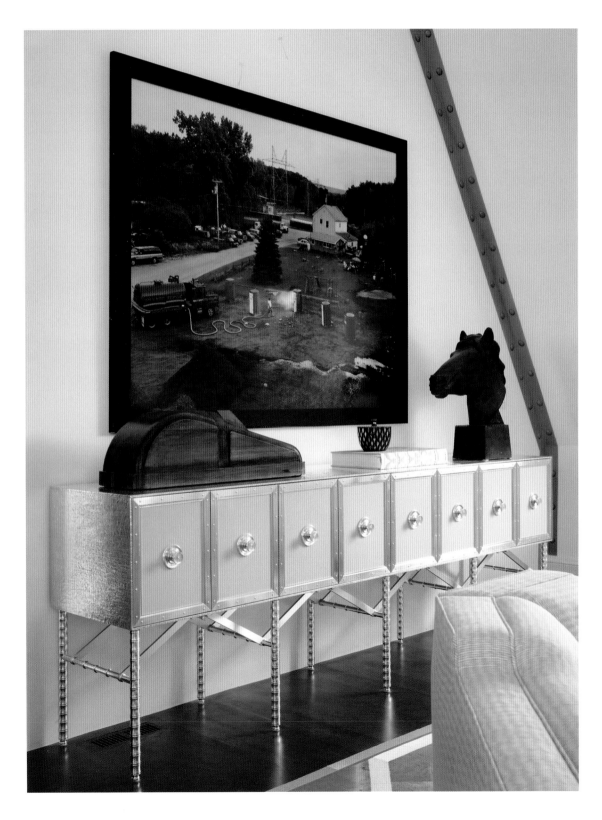

"Pairing the plush rug and buttery fabrics with tougher metal pieces creates a dynamic tension."

LEFT: One of our favorite collaborators, San Francisco artist Paul Benson, made this incredibly cool turned-aluminum-and-lacquer sideboard by hand. **OPPOSITE:** We riffed on the oddly angled space with this isosceles-shaped nook. In keeping with our industrial inspiration, we designed a steel fireplace surround with a floating hearth. Richard Diebenkorn's *Five Aquatints with Drypoint* and Ray Johnson's *Greer Garson Collage* hang above the mantel.

"The handsome stairway to the reading loft doubles as shelving for favorite books and objects."

LEFT: I love how nature and machine meet in pink peonies atop a heavy gear table. OPPOSITE: A pair of Austrian secessionist burl elm-wood-and-leather chairs from Epoca flank the stairs to the loft. Two steel-and-leather barn doors slide to conceal the bookshelves or the entrances to the two bedrooms on either side.

UNABASHED
GLAMOUR

It's all about making an entrance. Glamour is about having the confidence to assert your style, whether it's inspired by Daphne Guinness or the Sex Pistols. The same applies to interiors. The glamorous room is not a wallflower. It has luxe finishes, sumptuous materials, jewelry, and sparkle. An elevated setting affects how you move through a room, how you hold yourself. As they say, if you can't sit down in your couture gown, then you don't sit down.

Glamour can also be found in a gesture—the way someone lights a cigarette or throws on a coat. It's a bronze stair rail that invites a caress or a lounge chair that inspires a rakish pose.

The projects in this chapter are sophisticated and seductive. They have a bit of theatricality but stop short of going over the top. They feature finishes with depth, reflective surfaces, and luxurious fabrics like cashmere, velvet, and leather. They set the stage for a frisson, a soirée, or, let's face it, anything French!

Speaking of making an entrance, I'd love to have seen Babe Paley sweep down this grand foyer staircase. Its more traditional lines might give it a prim posture, but its gracious atmosphere and light-filled spaces imbue it with ease and elegance.

This residence is home to a young family with an appreciation for antiques. People often ask, "How do you make a traditional home feel current?" Well, that's exactly what we did here, juxtaposing classic and modern patterns, furnishings, and artwork. In the living room, a Louis XV–style commode and antique mirror are paired with a Sherie´ Franssen abstract painting; it's just the mix of modern and antique that I love. The walls are hand-stenciled, and the molding is glazed to create old-world charm and sheen.

The master bedroom centerpiece is a white Carrara marble fireplace whose curvy lines extend into voluptuous stone urns. And what could be more glamorous than a mirror ball? I like to imagine Ms. Paley might find this a perfect spot to enjoy a smart cocktail before making her entrance. Cheers, Babe.

"Contemporary artwork can ground a more traditional space in the now."

PREVIOUS PAGES: Sinuous curves bring glamour to the entrance and a baroque vignette. We divided the room with a path that leads to the French doors, a perfect spot to take in the view. **LEFT:** A marriage of old and new: A shapely antique French urn lamp and traditional wing chair converse with Sherie´ Franssen's dynamic work. The top of the coffee table is a nineteenth-century English chinoiserie serving tray. **OPPOSITE:** Above the hearth is Joshua Meyer's *Making Progress*—I hope we did its title justice.

PREVIOUS PAGES: The floral fabric that upholsters the chair was the starting point for this room—the client loved it, and so we incorporated its blue-and-orange palette throughout the space. **OPPOSITE:** Because the powder room is a small, discrete space, it offers an opportunity for over-the-top glamour. Here, we created a jewel box in vivid Hermès orange with a fanciful branch motif. **BELOW:** A range of mocha tones creates a sophisticated atmosphere in the study. We wrapped the walls and ceiling in Phillip Jeffries graphite hemp, hung taupe linen drapes, and placed a khaki woven-wool-and-linen rug underfoot.

PREVIOUS PAGES: The bedroom establishes a tranquil mood for the master suite. BELOW: The floating world of the master bath unfolds in peaceful white and sky blue tones. The counters are Carrara marble, and the floor is a trefoil pattern. OPPOSITE: The restful palette of colors and materials extends into the bedroom sitting area.

Turn off the phone, order champagne, and place the Do Not Disturb sign on the door. This serene, monochromatic space was designed to be like a hotel suite you never want to leave. We wrapped the room in a foil-backed grasscloth that glimmers in the light of the fireplace. Gold, silver, and other metallic touches sparkle. And drop-dead-cool lounge chairs by Franco Albini are perfect for reclining in with the latest issue of *Vanity Fair.*

Of course, there had to be a fabulous bed—we designed one with an eight-foot-by-eight-foot channeled headboard upholstered in woven gray tweed. And what self-respecting suite doesn't have a sharp bar? The pièce de résistance is a hand-hammered aluminum bar cart that is utterly 007-worthy (the Roger Moore Bond, naturally).

BELOW: Sumptuous materials and textures make this a sensual space. OPPOSITE: Those are not my gams in the Katy Grannan photograph.

"A bedroom should always be a haven of comforting textures, from top to bottom."

LEFT: Look up: a graceful hand-painted ceiling completes the room. **OPPOSITE:** Who wants turndown service when the bed is this divine? We dressed it in custom bedding made from sumptuous cashmere and merino wool and topped it with emerald-cut custom-embroidered pillows.

"I love a cocktail in the bedroom and a spa in the bath."

LEFT: Bespoke bar cart by Paul Benson set with Moser tumblers and bar accessories. **OPPOSITE:** The cross-shaped tile pattern in the master bath continues the geometric motif of the bedroom fabrics.

My dear friend Angelina has a portrait of herself in the living room. In glitter. It goes without saying that the girl likes her glamour. The owner of a chic Pacific Heights spa—which I also had a blast designing—Angelina wanted this home to be her own oasis. We began by primping her ladylike two-story town house with pink, chocolate brown, and Wedgwood blue paint. Redolent of old Hollywood, the living room called out for sexy, feminine pieces like a mohair daybed, tufted-silk and Lucite benches, and a custom pink-and-blue glass mosaic fireplace surround.

The dining room was born for entertaining. Glorious evenings unfold under the vintage bubble-glass chandelier and pink ceiling when guests gather for dinner around the white lacquer table. After the last guest (typically me) has finally made his exit, Angelina retires to her bedroom, kicks off her Jimmy Choos, and turns off the lamp—the one sitting on the enchanting mirrored 1930s bedside table, of course.

BELOW: Angelina—and her living room—are all about spirited femininity.
OPPOSITE: The curves of the fabulous arched windows are carried into the lines of the furniture, such as the svelte dining room table and chair.

"Glamour has more than one face—day or night, Angelina can relax in style."

PREVIOUS PAGES: The daybed is the perfect spot for a gossip session before an evening out. **LEFT:** A cozy corner for self-reflection. Portrait by René Garcia Jr. **OPPOSITE:** We wanted Angelina's bedroom to be restful without losing the glam factor. We choose dreamy blue as the backdrop for a custom Moroccan-inspired headboard and vintage mirrored side table.

This grand old gal needed a kick in her step. We sought to preserve the soul of this elegant English Tudor, designed by noted San Francisco architect Houghton Sawyer in 1913, while giving her new life. The spirited family of six that lives here also added an injection of energy.

Glamorous gestures set the scene in this storybook setting. In the foyer, you're met by a gracious stairway and stunning original woodwork. Crossing the hand-stenciled threshold floor, you enter a parlor that subverts the old-fashioned with fresh prints and chic silhouettes, like those of the 1940s French scrolling plume armchairs.

The master bedroom is an urbane retreat. While the palette is quiet, geometric graphics create visual interest, from the grid in the Tai Ping carpet to the ticking stripe of the wall covering. Standout pieces include a pair of Belgian leather chairs, a celestial 1960s crystal starburst chandelier, and a custom JDG-designed platform bed.

We're proud to say that we transformed this grande dame from dowager to doyenne. Now all she needs is to meet a nice young man.

BELOW: We designed this space to offer multiple conversation areas. The built-in banquette and custom JDG-designed seven-foot ottoman create a great space for relaxing with friends. OPPOSITE: A pair of Dennis & Leen high-backed English-style wing chairs define a more formal gathering place.

"Playful prints and artwork give formal a fresh new life."

LEFT: Decorative painter Willem Racké enlivened the walls with a fanciful branch motif. **OPPOSITE:** A 1930s Italian art deco glass chandelier casts a glamorous glow over Therien & Co.'s dining table and chairs. Kiki Smith's avian sculpture perches in the branches.

OPPOSITE: The space flows from family room to kitchen; the custom JDG breakfast table is complemented by Frances Adler Elkins chairs. BELOW: With the doors swung open to the terrace, this is a lovely, breezy spot for relaxing with family and friends.

BELOW: Once the kids are put to bed, it's time to head to the grown-up playroom—the media room and wine cellar—where the seating can easily be moved to make room for a DJ and dance floor. OPPOSITE: We designed the custom wine cellar; the backlighting from the racks adds an amber glow to the room.

OPPOSITE: A pair of vintage leather chairs and a contemporary mirror from Coup d'Etat; a Tai Ping wool-and-silk rug. Phillip Jeffries grass-cloth wall covering.
BELOW: Custom JDG-designed platform bed with inset Holland & Sherry headboard fabric. Zimmer & Rohde woven flax linen back pillows with Samuel and Sons cord trim.

"With its rich blues and browns, this space exudes masculine glamour—it's Steve McQueen as a room."

This room achieves its timeless style by bringing together a range of periods, from a late-eighteenth-century German neoclassical fruitwood commode to a 1960s Austrian crystal starburst chandelier to a contemporary Ralph Pucci chair and ottoman.

BELOW: In the master dressing room, the frame detail of the wardrobe is picked up in the etched glass doors. OPPOSITE: The custom vanity continues the motif.

CASUAL CHIC

What's better in life than casual chic? Informal and comfortable but pulled together and stylish, casual chic is the décor equivalent of brunch. The scale can be grand or intimate; just give me plush spaces for curling up, stacks of design books for inspiration, and art for the gaze (and yes, a discreetly hidden big screen for watching *Moulin Rouge!* on lazy Sunday afternoons).

In California, we're a town-and-country culture. We spend our weeks in the city and escape on the weekends to Sonoma, Napa, Tahoe, and Palm Springs. Lucky enough to be situated by the ocean, amid rolling hills and lush vineyards, we're also all about indoor/outdoor living. The homes in this chapter reflect that lifestyle. Think materials with a sense of ease, such as linen and cotton, prints that bring nature inside, and family heirlooms lovingly displayed. The look can be rustic or polished, but it has to be comfortable.

My husband and I have a small home in wine country, where no one worries about putting a glass directly on the table and nothing is too precious. I relish weekends there with good friends, our dog, Kingsley, and walks to our favorite local restaurant, Cook, for cocktails. It doesn't get any better than that. Love is the best accessory!

St. Helena is a little wine-country town where you know your favorite shop is open when the owners have hung out their sign at the corner of Main and Adams. But it's also a hot little destination: it's home to great restaurants, the Napa Valley Film Festival, and Auberge du Soleil. It's chic and relaxed at the same time—the perfect weekend getaway for my husband and me.

When we bought this St. Helena home, our real estate agent affectionately dubbed it the pool house, because it's the size of most of my clients' cabanas. It was a generic ranch house, built in 1962, but it backed up to a vineyard and had a great yard. We knew it had potential.

My homes are always my design labs, so I challenged myself with this project by working in a palette of cool whites and grays. (I haven't had white walls in my own home in fifteen years!) I wanted to create something relaxed but modern, so we used rustic materials but in unexpected ways: I designed a reclaimed-wood wall in a chevron pattern, for example, and we worked with Austin-based Howl Interiors on a moody fireplace surround made from blackened oyster shells.

Nothing makes us happier than pulling into the driveway—in Bea, as we call our vintage Grand Wagoneer woody—to spend the weekend. Now all the house needs is the pool.

BELOW: Wine country is all about indoor/outdoor living, so we installed sixteen-foot glass doors in the front and back of the house. **OPPOSITE:** The fireplace is the perfect spot to cozy up on a cool evening or after a brisk morning at crush, the annual wine-country grape-pressing ritual.

"The backyard abuts a vineyard, and we wanted to bring the mustard-flower palette indoors, hence the pops of yellow throughout."

The living room is inviting and relaxed, perfect for gatherings—any of the chairs can be drawn up to the fireplace, the sofa, or the table.

BELOW: I love pairing organic and refined elements in a space, like this gorgeous cluster of resin spheres, evocative of caviar (top center). **OPPOSITE:** The sinuous curves of the chair create a juxtaposition with the rustic wood wall.

1001 WHISKIES
YOU MUST TASTE BEFORE YOU DIE

SECRETS OF THE
SOMMELIERS

EDITH HEAD

PARIS

DRINK
THIS

BITTERS

"The kitchen is casual but crisp. It transitions seamlessly from a tranquil spot for morning coffee to a smart space for entertaining."

PREVIOUS PAGES: Michael's collection of vintage creamware is displayed in controlled chaos. **OPPOSITE:** In the kitchen, white and black geometric shapes create great graphic pop. **RIGHT:** For the closets throughout the house, we chose to keep it casual by using drapes instead of doors. The taupe-and-gray fabric and black window frame continue the color story in the guest room.

"Of course, the last thing you want when baring all your flaws is attention, so I thought the spotlights were a witty touch—sadistic but witty."

LEFT: The mirrors have crowns etched in the top, and I hung them so that when we look into them, the crowns rest on our heads. **OPPOSITE:** Stripes are one of my all-time favorite patterns—the guest bedroom is a panoply of handsome banding. **FOLLOWING PAGES:** A spot for enjoying the breeze or a good read. In the master bedroom, I had a striped blanket that we brought back from Morocco made into the headboard. I love that it looks like figured wood.

This stately white colonial is like a Connecticut summer home transported to California. Nestled in an enclave that is also home to such historic properties as the Carolands and the Tobin Clark estate, the house, with its 1920s-style architecture, called for tradition and elegance. But as home to a lively family, it also needed to be colorful and livable. For inspiration, we sought to channel a little bit of Albert Hadley and imbue classicism with joie de vivre.

The furnishings have a formal-but-lived-in quality befitting a summer home, as if they've been there for generations (and seen many rounds of Pimm's Cups). In fact, when designing the living room, the client seated himself on the sofa and stretched out his legs so we could determine the perfect ottoman height for resting his feet. And to complete the picture, the family recently acquired the perfect finishing touch: a charming little pup.

THE *Well*-LIVED LIFE

FLORANOVA   WARWICK ORME

"People say that sometimes a cupcake is just a vehicle for the icing. I think sometimes a side table is a vehicle for the cool stuff that sits on top."

PREVIOUS PAGES: This space is all about sherbet colors: the walls are swathed in lemony yellow, the ceiling in ice blue. **LEFT:** The console table by Studio Workshops displays a collection of personal objects. **OPPOSITE:** Joshua Meyer's *The Story of My Life* (which reminds the clients of their daughter) hangs above the custom settee that's designed to be perfect for story hour. **FOLLOWING PAGES:** The dining room has classic formality, but the contemporary art and fresh colors keep it from feeling staid.

BELOW: An homage to Lilly Pulitzer. The psychedelic tweeds on the armchairs are by Galbraith & Paul and Osborne & Little, and the drapes are in a blue, green, pink, and gold oyster linen by Raoul. The custom clover ottoman is in a gorgeous coral Victoria Hagan fabric. OPPOSITE: Tomato red high-gloss paint and a Galbraith & Paul printed linen enliven two pairs of vintage chairs. We had an easy-to-maintain, family-friendly tabletop made from recycled glass fabricated for the kitchen table. FOLLOWING PAGES: These warm, lively spaces are décor Prozac. How could you not feel cheerful surrounded by these colors?

This weekend retreat has a grand feel because of its proportions, but as a getaway in Sonoma, it's a place for everyone to decompress. For its jet-setting owners, we created an elegant interior that doesn't take itself too seriously, from the boldly striped pool house to my favorite piece in the home: a wonderfully eccentric deer-head chandelier (made of wood, people).

European rustic is what's expected in wine country; instead, we sought a fresh take on Sonoma style. To start, instead of the customary deep reds and greens, we upholstered furnishings in persimmon, yellows, and citrusy greens. We also strove to bring the glorious outdoors inside while uprooting traditional wine-country clichés.

OPPOSITE: I love the hands-free clock face—no one keeps track of the time in wine country. BELOW: This room was made for entertaining; the seating areas are flexible and can be easily rearranged.

"In Sonoma, what's inside should be just as verdant as what's outside."

LEFT: Man imitates nature, from the root table lamp by Ironies to the floral Lee Jofa fabric. **OPPOSITE:** The 1940s Italian verre églomisé mirror has reverse-painted gilt leaves. **FOLLOWING PAGES:** We originally wanted to tent this space in silk, but in a pool house, that would be a bit impractical. Instead, we replicated the look with custom decorative painting. This sunny yellow sitting room is the perfect spot to curl up for an afternoon nap.

"Casual places to drink and dine … and drink. After all, it's not called seltzer country."

LEFT: These are spaces tailor-made for wine flights. **OPPOSITE:** Walnut refectory dining table; eight custom-carved Louis XIII side chairs from C. Mariani slip-covered in an Osborne & Little linen-and-wool fabric. **FOLLOWING PAGES:** I think Bacchus would approve of the seating in this sunny guest bedroom. The grape colors in the master suite are a modern riff on wine-country hues.

This Los Angeles residence—home to pro skateboarder Reese Forbes and his wife, Shawn—is meant for living large. This is where Reese takes off down the perilously steep driveway on his latest deck while Shawn contemplates her next joyride in Tawny Kitaen, their nickname for their beloved tan Mercedes SL convertible.

Architecturally, the house already told a story: midcentury cool by way of the 1960s. With a nod to the Palm Springs and Palm Beach interiors of the era, we blended vintage and contemporary, sleek and ornate. In the living room, we kept things groovy with basket chairs, a white mohair rug, and a stack of floor pillows for impromptu seating. In the lounge, an outrageous mix of patterns rules.

Since we completed the project, Reese and Shawn have transitioned from rock-and-roll couple to parents (without losing their cool), and I love knowing we created a home that evolved with them.

"The living room
is a swingin'
hot spot. The
freestanding
fireplace allows
the party to flow
on all sides."

LEFT: We upholstered a
contemporary club chair with
a retro-inspired floral fabric.
OPPOSITE: A 1960 Aldo Tura
lacquered-parchment bar cart is
outfitted for old-school cocktails.

"The eclectic mix of vintage finds and modern pieces in this living room makes for a space full of personality, just like its owners."

Guests love to kick back in this pair of wire basket chairs; set on a white faux-fur rug, they're a fun nod to the sixties. And with the great view of the L.A. hills through the picture windows, who wouldn't feel groovy sitting here?

OPPOSITE: In Reese's study, it's ironic masculine iconography all the way, from the shield to the pipe to the framed "forebears." BELOW: The layering of vivid prints creates great drama in the sitting room.

"This room is the epitome of casual chic for me. Comfortable but stylish and cheerful without being precious."

The master bedroom is swathed in goldenrod yellow, providing a vivid backdrop for the sculptural winged headboard by JDG and the scroll bench.

ACKNOWLEDGMENTS

So many people to thank. This book, my design firm, the life I live would be so incredibly boring if I had to do it all alone.

Collected Cool would not exist without my right hand—no, my right arm—at JDG, principal designer Kelly Hohla. You have touched most of the interiors in this book. Your talent, support, friendship, and work ethic are bar none. You make me a better designer, and I look forward to many more years of collaboration. Plus, I would be a hot mess without you.

My husband, Michael, who inspires and encourages me always, who dresses me sometimes and who makes me laugh a lot. You are a great talent and Cavalier would not exist if it weren't for you. Come what may.

Miss Alisa Carroll, publicist, writer, and lover of all things black—thank you for the many years of dedication, collaboration, and making me sound very smart on paper. This book is yours as well.

My book team: Jill Cohen, that fateful water taxi into Venice was the beginning of our book discussions. Who knew then that little ol' me would have this amazing anthology of my work. And special thanks to Alisa Carroll (again), Doug Turshen, David Huang, Kathleen Jayes, and everyone at Rizzoli.

The best team in the business—JDG through the years—you have all been a part of this journey, and I appreciate each one of you. You have created wonderful memories and made me look like a star at all times (which I love): Dana Short, Molly Hildebrand, Jenn Sharp, Andy Reid, Chelsea Lund, Gennifer Yoshimoto, Suzanne Andrews, Natalie Gale, Emilie Munroe, Jill Judd, Meg Bucci, Kim Betzina, Coco Clark, Emily Mughannam, Alana Dorn, Travis Phillips, Alexis Ring, Jennifer Andresen, Katy Congdon, Lindsay Gerber, Timothy McGregor, and Cecile Lozano. And in loving memory of Chris Lytle, my first assistant and good friend, who is no longer with us.

To Richard Witzel, who gave me a real education in design. Richard took me to showrooms, client meetings, installations—everywhere he went, I went. It was an education not many young designers receive. His best advice: "Always remember, no matter the client or the project, you are always shopping for your own home at the same time!"

To Jamie Drake, my other design idol. You have showed me how to be a rock star and maintain dignity and poise with just a hint of irreverence.

To my ladies: I am thankful for the incredible support of some amazing women who have been in my life for many years—advising, laughing, referring clients, drinking, eating, imparting great wisdom: Angelina Umansky, Lisa Chadwick, Mary Lou Castellanos, Susan Chastain. I love you all!

I would be nowhere without clients who believed in our vision and took a risk with JDG: R & V, Mike, Shauna, Brad, Emily, Karl, Holly, Gary, Kathie, Seth, Angie, Lena, Sara, Christina, Graham, Brad, Ginger, Kevin, Nicole, JP, Beth, Brian, Hollie, Shawn, Reese, Mary Lou, Angelina, Galina, Ron, Tracy, Peter, Cara, Anita, Anne, Jim, Laura, Eugene, Stacy, Alison, Josh, Jessica, Stephen, Patti, Terrill, John, Sarah, Diane, Kathryn, Donna, David, Jeff, James, Diana, and Noel.

To my dog, Kingsley—JDG greeter, Cavalier mascot, and classic American beauty—love ya.

To all of you—I am eternally grateful.

First published in the United States of America in 2014
by Rizzoli International Publications, Inc.
300 Park Avenue South
New York, NY 10010
www.rizzoliusa.com

PHOTOGRAPHY CREDITS:

Joe Fletcher: 2; 131-139; 215-225

Matthew Millman: 3-8; 10-11; 15-33; 35-47; 49-55; 57-63;
65-83; 84-91; 95-109; 111-129; 141-145; 186-187; 190-195;
199-213; 227-239

Cesar Rubio: 149-163; 165-171; 173-179

Mark Darley: 181-185; 188-189

Michel Arnaud: 241-249

Jay Jeffers: 251

Front cover: Matthew Millman

Back cover: All photos by Matthew Millman except lower right
photo by Joe Fletcher

Endpapers: All photos by Matthew Millman

2014 2015 2016 2017 / 10 9 8 7 6 5 4 3 2 1

Distributed in the U.S. trade by Random House, New York

Printed in China

ISBN-13: 978-0-8478-4095-3

Library of Congress Catalog Control Number: 2013948613

Art Direction: Doug Turshen with David Huang